God's Little Dreamer

God's Little Dreamer

A Prayerful Book of Poetry

MEREDITH THOMAS

RESOURCE *Publications* • Eugene, Oregon

GOD'S LITTLE DREAMER
A Prayerful Book of Poetry

Resource Publications
An Imprint of Wipf and Stock Publishers
199 W. 8th Ave., Suite 3
Eugene, OR 97401

www.wipfandstock.com

PAPERBACK ISBN: 978-1-7252-8193-6
HARDCOVER ISBN: 978-1-7252-8194-3
EBOOK ISBN: 978-1-7252-8195-0

Manufactured in the U.S.A.   08/14/20

I would like to dedicate this book to my father on Earth.
He has truly loved and helped me.

Contents

He Is

Enfold me in Your arms.
I need love.
Wait. . .don't look.
It's too raw, as You press me to Your breast and I speak.
I speak of all that concerns me.
What I hate and what I'm thankful for.
Show Yourself a Prince Who will guide me and never let me go.
Let me swim in Your clean ocean of Mercy.
Let's sing together as I wash Your feet with all the bitter tears I've cried.

What's inside Your head?
This frustrates man.
Once like us, but not like us.
So succinct.
So wise.
How do You free Yourself in merriment?
I want to know what makes Your heart leap.

Let me dwell in Your piercing eyes and sleep.
Your hands are the hands of pure love.
Always outstretched in my mind.
Bare feet.
Roses about the heart.
Chunks of flesh jerked out of Your back.
Betrayed and despised.
God being spit on and mocked.
I don't understand this kind of love.

To what shall one compare Jesus to?

Maybe I overheard one say, "a lion with the heart of a lamb."

Please speak to me, whatever You are. . .don't leave me this way.

Mercy

Praise the Lord Who preserves me from insanity,
For it is a small thing for Him!
Let my heart be ever upon Him.
May He love others through me.

He said that He asks for so little.
May I give Him a lot!
When I hug a stranger, I am hugging Him.

I am naked before Him.
His eyes pierce me to tears because He knows the deepest parts of me.

Lord, in Your kindness,
Have mercy on me.
You fashioned me and know that I love Your ways and seek Your path,
Though it be narrow.
You know that I'm weak.
I have been humbled.

Lord, have mercy on me!
Man has little mercy to spare,
For man is quick to anger.
But You are kind.
Like David,
I'll take your wrath instead of man's.

He Beheld His Child

Things could have been a lot worse.
It is Your Will.
You drew me to Your bosom.
My eyes beheld the dust.
You saw misshapen clay.
You took some of the fire from my mind and placed it in a heart that was hollow.
To burn for You and wait for Your touch
Is oven-sweet misery,
Far better than the former pain.

You saved me from bitterness personified.
Is that love?
The very thought of You as my umbrella struck me like a lightning bolt.
Is that love?
You removed false prophets and the like from my life.
You gave me fresh eyes.
Is that love?
You speak through my earthly father to keep me from the Final Farewell.
Is that love?
One can only grow in Your love.

It's hard to give You crumbs while I'm hurting.
Lemon peels instead of wine.
I will get drunk in the blood from Your wounded side.
My back is against the wall,
But You kissed my life.

Clinging

When I look upon a rose, I imagine the hand that so tenderly placed each petal.
This is the same hand that struck the proud enemies and laid flat empires.
A hand so mighty as to cause a strangled cry from a nation.
Or to cause liberation and protection, as to make one weak with relief.

Let the bastard sons of Satan forsake a lovingly crafted bouquet of roses.
They like to be drunk with the strong perfume of Jezebel.
Let her scent grow stronger until they choke on the scent of iniquity.

As for me, I want the subtle scent that I must search for.
To bend in Your garden and be rewarded by the scents of what You've made.
What shall I fashion for You?

A heart that loves sincerely.
A heart that forgives.
A heart that loves to serve.
A heart that is full of song.
A heart that has survived pain but remains close to You.

Love me deeply, Father.
I crave a kiss from You on my cheek.
Touch my hand when I sleep, and protect me in that world too.

Thank You for Waiting

Mental pain runs like poison through my veins and paralyzes me.
What is it that eventually unlocks me?
Love or prayer?
They go hand in hand.
Jesus has assigned many people to pray for me.
He will bring me through this with joy.

I was told to sit in the torture chamber. . .
Thoughts racing.
No solutions.
I remind myself of His promise.
I feel Him present.
A calming word or two from Him is that shot that they need so desperately
    in the veins.
I'll need some more later, dear God.

Blessed are those who cling to His bosom daily.
Cursed are those who despise His ways.
Do you think that your back won't be up against the wall one day?

I want to see us smile together, my new, dear friend of my heart's imagination.

You need a real friend and so do I.

Depth and velvet substance wrapped around you.

Finally, I can sit with someone without needing a dictionary for things like sympathy,

And the laughter can flow without having to dig it out of the freezer and letting it thaw.

Thank You, Lord, for the manifestation of blessings.

A friend of my flesh was given to me.

Torn Alive

My heart is torn in two.
Still connected and beating.
God, why don't You run Your finger along the split?
Don't push it back together.
I will not desire a heart filled with fake smiles and mediocre feelings.
And weak compassion because it wasn't properly healed. . .like some mis-
    guided counselor.

A torn heart.
A cracked egg.
And all the while my love for You is being tested.
Just remember, Job was a man and I am not.

"Let her learn to smile with a broken heart, and to see that I keep it intact
So that she should know how not to treat my other children who are broken
    and in pain.
To desire to save the children from ignorance of the Father of all Hope. . .
The only way out of misery.
May she have visions of souls destined for My embrace,
But must wait
And cry countless tears with no means to help herself.
May she realize the importance of prayer and how it draws her close to My
    bosom.
Let her rant against Me and then humble herself in her wretched state.
I will not bleed her dry.
My love will heal her and chase those demons away."

She's a Song

Bead by bead,
I climb to my salvation.
I need a billion beads to make it all right.

Did you know that Jesus and I sip coffee together?
That He likes it spicy?
He asked me, "Child, where's the love?
You can share the Stigmata, sweetheart, but you must forgive."
I took a sip.
He clutched me closer to His bosom.
He drank half the cup. Cinnamon, allspice, cayenne.
Cinnamon is His favorite.
He set the cup down.
My heart slowly closing its center together.
I didn't try to stop it at first. A test. I spoke.

"Jesus, I choose it with every rosary for her. I open myself up too much. My
      entrails. . ."
"My entrails were exposed too, dear heart. My arms wide open."
I grabbed the cup of coffee.
I thought that I needed CBD oil.
The coffee was lukewarm.
I looked into His eyes.
They smiled as our minds connected about the Scripture.
I pretended that I was going to spit it out and then gulped it down.
Jesus laughed.

I sat the cinnamon-tainted cup down and wanted my love…as always…tangible.
He tapped me on the forehead,
Then He tapped me on the heart.
"They must meet."
He spoke with authority.
"How is that even possible?
When you know they don't want to connect?

I despise her in the inner heart.
You have nothing to say to those quick to conflict,
Yet they will say it was I who struck the first blow."
I felt it come on me.
I beat His strong, broad chest three times before laying my head against His heart and sobbing And screaming.
He continued holding me.
Did He get warmer?
I sweated just a bit.
I looked at the only light that flickered in the room,
The light of the candle of Our Lady of Guadalupe.
Barely flickering. New candle. New relationship with her.

Jesus was there, yet
I was no longer in His embrace.
Just a girl in a tattered, blue chair with an empty cup of coffee.

"Write her song! We will begin that way.

You love music.

Love her."

These thoughts that He put in my head made me tingle. Solid. Brick foundation for a change.

I thanked the Lord.

He gets me. . .always.

If I Knew

I don't understand Your mercy.
I don't understand Your forgiveness.
I don't understand Your love.
You loved me first, so I love You.

You wrote a story called Life
And put me in it.
Please highlight me in every page because I acknowledge You,
And You know that it is in a special way.

Bead after bead.
Tear after tear.
Fear after fear.

We give so many pieces of ourselves to the wrong people.
I know I did,
And I'm learning
To be stingy
And give more time to You.
To be consumed. . .

I'm always wanting to be the twinkle in Your eye
And more.
The baby You adore.
Because You're my Daddy.
And You know the struggle
Between the natural and supernatural.
You don't despise the tender bits and pieces of my child's heart.

You're Really Something, You Know

Nothing is hard for You.
How easy it is for things to be hard for me!
I know that David plays the harp.
Is it alright if Bing and I sing to You with piano keys?
Or with a band that's feather soft?

You're shiny.
Heaven is more than a glow of love,
But on Earth, it'll have to do.
They'll always be a light somewhere
As long as I'm with You.
So long to all the jokers I've met,
But they're Your people too.
Help me to love them. . .make it easier someway,
If that's part of loving You.

Love for the Father

Who is more beautiful than my Daddy?
Not even the Glorious Son!
Daddy's eyes are one million times bluer than sapphires.
They pierce the soul of saint and sinner.
Sharper than the sharpest sword.
Behold how He loves war!
More masculine than a billion Samsons and Davids,
And His peace is more intoxicating than drugs and wine.

I love my Daddy Who protects me.
We will laugh and sing.
His lap is my home.

Acknowledge the Lord

Let them laugh now, for they'll be weeping later.
The warm love of God is not in them.
Their blood, their life's blood,
Runs cold.
And they don't know why.
They don't recognize Satan's touch.

As for me,
God dances in my blood 'til I feel drunk.
He speaks to me.
He keeps me in good health and of a youthful appearance,
Because I worship my Father.
I like to know Him.
I like to paint Him.
I like to serve Him.

The Lord rewards those who love Him.
They will be like glasses of overflowing wine.
No pieces taped together limping through life,
For He will make them whole.

Oh, Daddy!

Speak to me, Daddy.
Please step off of Your throne.
I see the wind play across Your face,
Because You just felt like it.

Tell me why You love music.
What a wonderful thing to create!
Tell me why wine seems sacred.
I like the idea of it flowing through my blood.
Your voice is wine.

When I humble myself before You tonight,
I'll think of the time when I felt Your eye upon waking.

Daddy,
Let me not mix with fools.
They forever reject the truth.
Let us mend the broken,
For they are humble and reach for You.

Hold me to Your bosom forever,
Warming my blood until it sings,
So that I can sing of Your love and Your strength!

He Knows

Whisper sweet things to my soul,
And bring it to warm tears of relief.

I'm full of patterns that I don't understand.
The others try to force bricks together,
But You know the perfect amount of sunlight
To shine between the cracks.

You know when my temperature needs to be fixed.
You know what is crooked within me.
You know when the pipes up above are stopped up.

Yea; my Lord and Daddy knows me.
He birthed me to be His eternal treasure.
He didn't have to.

What's Next?

Father,
I am poor,
Weak,
Ignorant,
Angry,
Afraid,
Frustrated,
Meek,
Determined,
Devout,
Sorrowful,
Depressed,
Anxious,
Rejected,
Misunderstood,
Quiet,
Lonely,
And broken.
Have I died to self yet?
It's been a slow death.
Lava in the brain.
Werewolves scarred my heart.
I live.

Help from Daddy

Daddy,
Don't let me go when I run to You.
Press Your tingling hands into my head.
Clean it. Clean the crevices.
Remove the encrusted pieces of garbage.
Electric shocks of confusion,
Triggered by the slightest thing,
Yet You never despised me or my afflictions.

The Great Son of God said that we have to wait it out.
Wait for healing.
Wait for love.
Please send my true love
As a healing balm.
Drain me.

My Spotless Daddy-God

I play peek-a-boo in the folds of Your robe.
You laugh, and the thunders bow in fear.
I kiss Your strong and mighty hand.
You point to the Son.
I bow and kiss His feet.
I thank Him for reconciling us to You.
Is Your beard filled with power?
Your whole being is power mingled with unspeakable love.

Rock me to sleep with Your kisses on my cheeks
That cause my blood to start singing praises to You,
For You are perfect,
Without a stain.
From beginning to end.
Amen.

I Want Him to Myself

A Father Who will never neglect me.
I know that voids come and go.
Because You love me so,
That You can't bear to see me bored.
If I were to sit and imagine You in Heaven,
I could dream up some wonderful tales.
A buttercream colored background.

Various angels flying everywhere You go.
A golden throne,
That if it, or rather, just part of it,
Were to be on Earth,
It would melt the sun in a breath's length of time.
Just think: that's the power of my Daddy's throne.
What of Him. . .
Himself?

Only the Father knows about His great power!
The Father already knows what just the two of us will do together for all
    eternity.
I'm awfully stingy when it comes to my Daddy!

Daddy Slow

Precious pearls of silence are lacking.
Garbage thrown down a tunnel while I walk through it in slow motion,
Clinging to beads.
Where is my God?
Our love is precious.
I will press into Him: crying, screaming. . .
He doesn't mind.
Like me, He doesn't like to be forsaken and abandoned.
Or forgotten.

His footsteps are slow.
Does He want me to match His pace?
Oh, Lord, how much longer?

Things to Occur

Daddy,
My bones ache, and I'm worn out like those ready to perish.
Old before my time.
You are ancient but never grow old.
Your health is beyond my imagination.
The blood of Christ surges and dances,
Just happy to be in His veins.

May David put me to sleep with his harp.
May angels breathe on me as I sleep.
Christ, stick one finger into the center of my heart
And the other in the amygdala.
Heal me.

Kiss me like I'm Your baby.
I am.
May Daddy God press my face to His,
So that I will be beautiful.
May I drink the blood of the saints.
It's so indescribably delicious and sweet.
Then, suddenly my blood hums throughout me.
God, may my vison quickly form into something like a garden.

I'm of Him

I cling to Your robe.
We cannot be apart for a second.
I want to swim in Your gorgeous eyes.
They inspired the creation of the sea.
Come, let us be one in some way.
Pierce my hands and kiss my soul.
Lock me up tight inside of You,
For I know I'm Your treasure.
Love me most of all.
I need it.

We're so much alike in ways.
I am no God, but I take after my Father.
I don't want to be God.
I want to be loved passionately by the Highest.
Come, put my crown of thorns in storage.
When You pierce my hands,
You touch me.
I love You, Daddy.
You know what I mean in everything.

Father Artist

You fashioned St. Uriel, the archangel.

To Him I ask for the juices to keep flowing.

He and I are friends who understand that Father loves through art.

Brushing the blue sky with white strokes.

Fashioning foxes with wings.

The glow of the sun dancing and resting in a clear jug of water.

Too many things He has done to inspire His little ones!

Let me love You with a portrait or a song.

Conversations are not often the way He says, "I love you."

The Need

You told me to shake the dust from the leaves.
My mouth is full of dirty leaves and my fingers stick together.
You shake Your mighty head,
Knowing that I can't dislodge a grudge without Your help.
It is impossible.
The foul princes are masters of torment and pain.
Spinning the same tune.
Giving dreams of them producing lava from my cracked skull.
Where is my embrace with one pierced hand holding the healing balm of love?
"Oh, man, how you put such little faith in Me!"
Father, please understand that we dwell in the land of sorrows.
Clawing blindly into the air for Your love and Your face.

Moments with You

If there is a disconnect, I feel it.
You want me to reflect on what to do.
You want to be praised.
I praise God because flies look like little raisins.
The sun's heat brings water out of my body,
Yet without its touch, nothing would burst forth into life and grow.
You've laid green carpet beneath my feet.
Little dots of light in the sky are prettier than jewels.
The light decides what's beautiful.
Everything that is
Is because of You. . .somehow and some way.

Speak

I'm weary, and I don't mince words.
In Jeremiah, You spoke poetry.
My God is a poet.
His skill flows effortlessly.
Speak poetry to my bones.
Awaken me with Your subtle ways of saying how You love me.
May Your Holy Spirit overtake me,
Caressing my very being.
I pray to You.
Please speak to me.

Wading Through

You were never born.
You told a saint, "I Am He Who Is. She is not."
You told me that one must die to self if one is to be Your child and follower.
I've had my share of blows that nearly killed me.
I've begged for death, yet You held me up.
Through muck and mire, I still breathe.
Help me to breathe for You.

Great Daddy

How much larger and stronger is Your mind compared to ours?
My mind is lower than an infant's compared to Yours.
I like that You smile upon me.
Earthly highs are crumbs from Satan
Compared to Your Divine Presence.

We don't understand.
We ought not to pretend that we do.

I'll listen and take advice from saints,
But I am a newborn lamb in Your eyes.
To one day see the Father's eyes of love,
Tenderly gazing upon me,
Will be the ultimate encounter.

Place me upon Your lap. . .the Great Daddy.
The color of Your robe might somehow be whiter than white.
Somehow softer than silk.
Your embrace will be warmer than the sun.
Yet, I shall gladly bear it.

That beautiful face!
I want to grab it and shower it with kisses!
Let's sing to one another about the time
I felt You breathe through me to remind me
How I belong to You and from where I get my every need and breathing too.

May my father on earth lead me to You.
To dance for You.
And then with You.
My big, beautiful Daddy!

Daddy, Teach. . .

Will a time come when I will despise to be honored in any way?
You have taught me so much about the importance of humility.
No one can rush my words to you.
I let the wind carry them.
May a cherub fly them to You.
There is an indescribable joy at knowing that I can't succeed without You.
It keeps You grounded as my Father, even though
Nothing can tie You down.

Remember in high school,
How I waited for the bus in the afternoons,
Trying to imagine You waiting too.
Waiting with me because I was lonely.
I would imagine You 6'2 with long brown hair,
A white robe, and a smile.
I was too wooden to talk to You
Or let You in.

Your heart is for the young.
You didn't like my pain.
You knew what was to come
And saw things of the air I dare not summon.
Jesus, You cherish the meek in spirit.
You forgive those who ignore You.

You know we are spotted clay.
I wonder about You still as I talk to You today.
May Your heart be surrounded by roses
For every tear I cry.

So Many Things

So many things I touch and taste
Are because of You.
I take everything for granted.
You, Who Are, are You Who Always Was.
Never birthed from some dark and secret womb.
Absolutely nothing created You.
I can't wrap my head around it, and I shudder at the thought of never having
    You.
I might as well have sprung from Your virginal loins,
For I'm so completely of You.
An odd thing to say, but true!
Rather, I was shaped by Your hands.
Your thought of me was filled with love,
Wanting me to love You in return.
Help me to love You more.

How Splendid is He!

Flying foxes!
How I delight in what You create!
A gate of pearls or one huge pearl?
Jewels are precious in Your sight.
May the righteous be like jewels of various sizes and shapes.

You are my Daddy.
You work hard.
Nothing makes You weary.
Let me feel Your Spirit resting with me!
You like dancing and singing.
You are sweeter than honey.
Your fist is much stronger than iron.
Your roar frightens the pit of hell.
But You are Precious in every way.

I'll See

So many things stick in my craw.
I feel like a carved-out pumpkin.
Where are You to make the proper arrangements?

So many people whom I need to forget.
In and out. . .in and out.
Is true friendship to allude me?
I don't feel bad complaining because I can't fool You.

Here's my entrails, let's clean it up.
Only God can clean any mess.
The Master Janitor for the righteous and then some.

Take Over

Fashion me an amygdala of gold.
A prefrontal cortex of steel.
Cool, clear thoughts like the purest stream.
Before I ascend to Heaven via natural death,
May I spit in every evil spirit's face, especially his.
I will humiliate Satan because I refuse to be his trophy.
I'm no fool to take on even his weakest minions.
I hide under feathers stronger than death.
My God is my shield like David said.
You will heal me and see me through for Your Name's sake.
Amen.

Great

Loosen the ties that bind me, and fasten me to a jewel on Your robe.

Praise the Lord Who sees the end of each earthly being's journey in this world.

His eye is strong enough to split your soul in two!

But He is filled with love and mercy,

The creator of the two.

They embrace one another.

The tiny, still voice is like a little candle in my soul.

May no voice of a heathen, including myself, snuff it out!

Consider Him

Fill me up Jesus, for I am weary.
So often humans are struck by fatigue.
We are so fragile compared to You.
When You showed me Your face,
Your blood-filled cheeks shamed the healthiest man!
How Your blood must dance and even praise You,
Yet You are God and not a mere human.

Jesus. . .the beautiful God Who became man.
But I know You are the Lord, and not a frail little creature like a human,
Especially me.
Bold eyes!
Bluer than the blue of Earth and piercing as the sharpest blades times infinity!
Cheeks carved high, yea; reminds me of what it says in Proverbs
About a bed of spices.

Your hair full with curls that crackle like fire.
A firm, kind mouth that is proper for a man.
The nose does not distract.

You were pruning sycamore trees.
You were pruning me.

Hold On

My coffee is nearly lukewarm.
Which one of us should spit it out on the ground?
Praise be to a God of passion!

He values the sufferings of His saints.
He often doesn't take shortcuts.
He sees us fuming and has compassion,
But it's hard to trust invisible hands to orchestrate things.

It seems as though I've swallowed too many bitter dregs, and that He's silently watching
With languorous lids. . .eyes too beautiful to behold.
He reminds me that He's my Father.
So, I needn't worry about how long the means stretch to the end.
Praise God for good surprises!

He Rewards

Praise God,
For He rewards endurance!
That still, quiet voice is the candle of hope inside of you.
Do not let the enemy snuff it out and make you hollow and barren like
A tree that He shall wither in Disgust.

Praise God Who gives us words to say in prayers,
As He guides us to safety in Him.
It is all in Him.
Love and life flow from His sacred veins.
I really can't imagine Him sitting still.
Maybe on a Sunday.

Pure Strength

What He says goes.
No trace of weakness like thinking to change His mind.
His throne is proud to belong to Him.
The Son kisses His hand.
Only God can be as alabaster and have unspeakable power.
Take solace in a Sovereign King of Kings.
Harder than rock.
Just think what He can do to His enemies!

Twinkle Twinkle

I'd like to think that His eyes twinkle when we thank Him.
Then again, I'm Irish.
A God for all races. . .never overwhelmed.
All patterns of thoughts are His design, spread well before Him.
Does God put a twinkle in my eye?
Yes, with hope for healing.
Because of Who He Is
And I who am not.

When I'm New

Will I have a different name in Heaven?
How many syllables?
Will the noise of it be like a burst of air?
The old name will be cast off, not even a memory.
There will be new textures and aromas.
I was content with coffee, vanilla, and silk.
My understanding will be open to all He wishes to share.
Praise be to a God Who is gracious and generous!
A God of joy Who delights at the sight of our little movements and voices.
I will know the texture of His arms when He holds me on His lap.

Refresh Me with You

Father, my flesh drags me through the day.
The sunshine and cerulean sky give me a boost.
A small accomplishment makes my heart dance.
A good rest and some coffee make me content.
If I study my blessings, I can smile for a while.

I long for Your Holy Spirit to have a holiday in every part of my inner being
    connected to You.
I want that heat that humbles and tingles.
The source known but unseen.
You love varying degrees of fire.

Passionate fire that heals and bestows love.
I'll take as much of that as I can.
I love to feel my God.
Just now, I pictured Your face covered by the wind
Like something that I must paint.

Honey God

The saints never run out of things to say about You.
Did I just hear You say, "Because of My mercy"?
Praise be to God!
A Divine Being Who is all power and merciful too.
Not like the satanic Greek gods,
A perverse figment of man's imagination.
If one of us were to rule, or the demons,
Sure, they would want to be You but not like You.
People crave power but are seldom merciful.
I'll pick the log out of my own eye.
You've been more than patient with me.
You are honey-sweet.

The Correct Song

Why are songs about You in my day silly and strange?
Casual clothes, guitars, and a stage?
If one is gifted with a truly beautiful voice like in the days of my father,
One should mainly sing Your praises.
Singing is a gift that they didn't give themselves.
A beautiful voice that sings about You
With an upside-down heart is no good.
It's like they're slapping us in the face.
If I could sing, perhaps I'd hide it from the evil world.
And sing when we're alone.
Would I run out of tunes for You?
No, because You're at the heart of everything that I do.

From the Trench

I'm entrenched in nonsense like that actor that I was
Bug-eyed over.
Head in the white fluffy clouds or the ones darker than
Pitch black.
Life is this.
A thunderstorm rages but only inside of my mind.
God lets rain pour down my eyes until I'm in the fetal position,
Wondering why He is no umbrella.

Sleep comes upon the joyful and the miserable.
I don't want to wake up,
But I do.
I open my eyes and cry out like a baby.
I count to sixty.
Eyes open.
He's rooted in me.
He moves with me as I dress, do laundry, paint,
And realize that I'm halfway through a day.

Red Blood

You put the red in my blood,
For You color my life.
It just takes a glow
To make the mission possible.
I start to think of everyday details and what could be,
Until it all forms into mountains in my way.
Just a ray of Your kindness clears the clutter away.
Unappreciated and exhausted.
Just a breath from You will grease the machine that I must be.
You see me as a lamb ever before Your glorious eyes.
My leaps and heartbeats are all in Your hands.

A Kiss

You kissed my vein,
And my blood was stirred.
I could praise You with strength up and down the streets!
How glorious is our God Who shed His perfect blood!
The Precious Man-God has blood like ruby lightning,
And Jesus is His name!

A Loving God

Praise the Lord Who answers prayers!
He smiles and laughs when sometimes we finally understand.
His laugh is hearty, but then there is a sound of many chimes.
Praise the Lord Who has many angels for many reasons!
He made them because they're very beautiful and obey gracefully.

God loves peace.
His peace is staggering to the dark ones.
They will never know it.
God will give portions of His peace to His true children.
God loves to give,
Because He is Love and the source of it.

Smiling Seas

He delights in the ocean.
It is like Him, for you can't control it,
Though He can and He does.

Sometimes I feel like I'm drowning.
The waves of life toss me about.
Situations and people I can't control.
An unkind word. . .

Crash!
I must try to reach the shore.
Surely, that's where His goodness is.
I've been tossed around too long.

There are dolphins here.
And the sun still shines, and the sky hangs low.
He tosses me a boogie board,
And I ride the waves.
Water is part of life.

Twirl

Twirl me around, and praise be to a God of dancing!
A God of mirth.
How You must love to laugh at us!
I'm of You, and so do I.

If only You carried a piece of the sky with You in one hand
And me in the other hand.

I crave Your Glory and Your beauty to be near to me.
Your thoughts are dear to me.
Oh, my loving Father, how tender You are to Your lamb!
I will praise a God of unspeakable love!
Hold me.
Tighter.

Crush the Snakes!

My longing for my God is great.
There are those who are proud to be snakes who can sit.
They refrain from sweetness and are bloated with salt.
Their beady eyes pretend many things.

You wonder where God is,
To smite them as you pass them by
While they withhold their kindness,
But treat you another way with their moods.

But God is great.
He is love and patience.
He will test the righteous.
He will wait to see if you exchange venom for venom.
If you turn into what you despise. . .

Best to be quiet.
Best to stay civil.
There is a right way.
One must forgive and pray.

Enfold Me

I feel a shade of blue.
Take me out of the shade and bring me to that warm palace in Your heart.
Let the sun kiss my cheek good morning.
You tease my hair with the wind.

You're great,
But just to feel Your special love
Makes life worth living.

When night comes
And the angels do their graceful dance,
Tuck me in with great care
And guard me through the sinister hours.
And then be my sunshine all over again.

With Light Shining Through

Gray or white,
Subdued or bright,
A color for every emotion I could hope to have.
You like them because You like to play with them.
You paint with them.
I'm sure You're pleased
At how the strokes help design the sky.
For without clouds,
The sun would grow lonely.
Praise be to God Who can puff up my clouds
With light shining through!

Constant Valentines

Praise the Lord Who fashioned the lamb!
Though days may be weary,
In Heaven He will gift you a little bird
With blueberry colored diamonds down its back
And roses painted on its wings.

For He loves you.
Sing at His feet in awe of His creation.
Does not His creation speak of love?

The whirling winds to refresh you with another season.
Notice the flowers as constant Valentines.
Notice, dear, but don't tarry in the garden of your thoughts.
Pray without ceasing, for He loves to talk with you.

Textures

I cannot think too much anymore.
I can only feel textures of love.

Velvet reassurance with a glow.
Soft nobs like heavy carpet for perseverance.
Stiff folds of cloth for endurance.
Metal chains against my skin for piety.

I imagine Your breath as warm against my skin
As You hold me to Your bosom.
Softer than silk is Your robe.
Solid as bricks are Your promises to me.
You've fashioned bricks of gold 'round me
For protection.
Amen.

Wait for His Peace

Chocolate covered days
And candy-coated daydreams.

Reality.
Painfully detailed
With no place to hide.

My God's robes move as He walks.
Everything that touches Him praises Him.
He needs no window to see me.
He knows my tears that touch His heart
Like raindrops against a window pane.

I call His name.
I need my Father's embrace.
He calms the sea and doesn't hide up above.
He's in every tender consolation.
God makes things right for those who wait.

Love Him

He upheld me.
I did not fall.
His angels are very gorgeous.
What must He look like?
I doubt if He has wings,
Though I try to have Him tell me things.
I will see Him all the time, perched upon His lap.

He is Love,
But He is just.
I will pay to the last penny, but
Purgatory has not escaped me in this life.
I still want Him,
And that's why He dotes on me.

A rose is beautiful.
It spirals inwards and grows thorns.
I will prick myself, and the blood will show
On my white wool,
For I am ever His lamb.

www.ingramcontent.com/pod-product-compliance
Lightning Source LLC
Chambersburg PA
CBHW061510040426
42450CB00008B/1555